A NOTE TO PARENTS

When your children are ready to "step into reading," giving them the right books—and lots of them—is as crucial as giving them the right food to eat. **Step into Reading Books** present exciting stories and information reinforced with lively, colorful illustrations that make learning to read fun, satisfying, and worthwhile. They are priced so that acquiring an entire library of them is affordable. And they are beginning readers with an important difference—they're written on four levels.

Step 1 Books, with their very large type and extremely simple vocabulary, have been created for the very youngest readers. **Step 2 Books** are both longer and slightly more difficult. **Step 3 Books,** written to mid-second-grade reading levels, are for the child who has acquired even greater reading skills. **Step 4 Books** offer exciting nonfiction for the increasingly proficient reader.

Children develop at different ages. **Step into Reading Books,** with their four levels of reading, are designed to help children become good—and interested—readers *faster.* The grade levels assigned to the four steps—preschool through grade 1 for Step 1, grades 1 through 3 for Step 2, grades 2 and 3 for Step 3, and grades 2 through 4 for Step 4—are intended only as guides. Some children move through all four steps very rapidly; others climb the steps over a period of several years. These books will help your child "step into reading" in style!

To Erin Gathrid,

who showed us the path,

and to

Lena Isabella Shefelman,

our first grandchild,

who will follow her own

Library of Congress Cataloging-in-Publication Data:
Shefelman, Janice.   A mare for Young Wolf / by Janice Shefelman ;
illustrated by Tom Shefelman.   p.   cm. — (Step into reading. A step 3 book)
SUMMARY: Teased for choosing a mare for his first horse, Young Wolf learns how to ride like a warrior.   ISBN 0-679-83445-1 (trade) — ISBN 0-679-93445-6 (lib. bdg.)
[1. Horses—Fiction.   2. Indians of North America—Fiction.]   I. Shefelman, Tom, ill. II. Title.   III. Series: Step into reading. Step 3 book.   PZ7.S54115Mar   1993
[E]—dc20   91-42749

Manufactured in the United States of America   10 9 8 7 6 5 4 3 2

STEP INTO READING is a trademark of Random House, Inc.

Step into Reading

A Mare for Young Wolf

By Janice Shefelman
Illustrated by Tom Shefelman

A Step 3 Book

Random House New York

1
Father's Gift

Young Wolf watched the horses eating the new grass. His father had many horses. He was the peace chief.

"I love all of you," Young Wolf said. "You are my gods."

The horses went on eating grass. All but one. She raised her head and turned her ears toward him.

"Nnnnn-hhhhh," she said. Her spirit entered his heart.

"You are the smartest, most beautiful one of all," said Young Wolf. "I will call you Red Wind, because your coat is red. And when you run, you are like the wind."

He picked some cottonwood leaves and fed her from his hand.

"See, Red Wind, we can be friends."

One day Eagle Feather summoned him.

"My son, you are old enough to have a horse of your own. Which one do you choose?"

Young Wolf's heart leaped.
"Red Wind," he said.

"Which one?" asked his father.

"The red mare with the golden mane and tail," Young Wolf answered.

Eagle Feather frowned. "Mares are for women and children—not for a warrior of the People. They do not make good war horses. Are you sure you want a mare?"

"Yes," said Young Wolf. "She is the most beautiful of all. And when I talk to her, she listens. I know she can learn."

Eagle Feather nodded. "Then she is yours."

"Thank you, Father."

Young Wolf went out to the horses. In one hand he carried a rope.

"Come, Red Wind. I have some leaves for you."

Red Wind took the leaves from his hand with her lips. She did not bite him.

"Now I will slip this loop over your head."

She kept on chewing.

He blew his breath into her nostrils. "Smell who I am," he said.

The mare flared her nostrils. She smelled Young Wolf.

"You are mine now," he told her.

Her ears turned to catch his words.

Young Wolf led her to the village.

"Look at my new horse, Mother!" he called.

Voice of the Sunrise was scraping a buffalo hide.

"She is a beauty, Young Wolf," she said.

Young Wolf smiled. "I know. And smart too."

Little Big Mouth came running up.
He looked at Red Wind and sneered.
"Only babies ride mares." He pointed at
Young Wolf and began to chant.

"Baby Wolf, Baby Wolf
Rides a mare.
Baby Wolf, Baby Wolf
Still goes bare."

His friend joined in. Other boys in the
village came to see what was happening.
Young Wolf's heart lay on the ground.

2

Grandfather's Lessons

The family sat around the fire eating their evening meal.

"I hate Little Big Mouth," said Young Wolf.

"Why?" Grandfather He-Bear asked him. "What did he do?"

"He said mares are for babies."

"I warned you," Eagle Feather said.

"Let Little Big Mouth talk," said his grandfather. "We will make Red Wind the best war horse in the village. Then you will have to guard her from the Apaches."

Young Wolf's heart soared.

"Yes, Grandfather. At night I will keep her beside our tepee tied to my arm. So no one can steal her."

"Good," said his grandfather.

In the morning Grandfather He-Bear began Young Wolf's lessons.

"Put your hands on her back and press down."

Young Wolf did as he was told.

"Now harder," said his grandfather.

Little Big Mouth and his friend watched.

"Ha, ha, ha! Look at Baby Wolf," they said.

"Your mouth is as big as a buffalo wallow!" Young Wolf yelled. "And your tongue is black!"

"Enough," said Grandfather He-Bear. "Listen to me, not them."

Young Wolf's heart was hot. "I will try, Grandfather," he said.

"Now let her feel your weight," his grandfather went on.

Young Wolf gave a little jump and clung to Red Wind's back.

"Like this?" he asked.

But Red Wind tossed her head. She reared up on her hind legs.

Young Wolf fell to the ground.

"Oh, buffalo chips!" he said.

He could hear the two boys laughing.

"Baby Wolf can't even ride a mare."

Young Wolf started toward them with his fists clenched.

But Grandfather He-Bear caught hold of his arm.

"No, Grandson. It is not manly to fight among ourselves."

"Little *Bad* Mouth is what he *should* be called," said Young Wolf.

"Be patient," his grandfather said. "Tomorrow we will try another way."

The next day Grandfather He-Bear said, "Run your hands over Red Wind's body."

Young Wolf stepped close to her.

"What if she kicks?" he asked.

"Talk to her."

"Hoh, Red Wind," said Young Wolf. "Make your legs like tree trunks."

He ran his hands over her back, along her sides, down her legs.

She moved sideways, away from him.

"Maybe she is afraid of me," he said.

"Show her there is nothing to fear," said his grandfather.

"How?" asked Young Wolf.

"You will think of a way."

3
Young Wolf's Idea

That night Young Wolf asked himself, "What can I do?"

He could hear Red Wind outside the tepee. She blew out through her nose and settled down to sleep.

"I know!" he answered himself. He crawled under the edge of the tepee.

"May I use your back for a pillow?" he asked Red Wind.

"Nnnnn-hhhhh," she said.

"I guess that means yes," said Young Wolf. He crawled closer.

"I am only a boy," he said. "You will hardly feel me." He laid his head on Red Wind's back.

"Nnnnn-hhhhh," she said, and put her head down.

Soon they were both asleep.

"Did you think of a way?"
Grandfather He-Bear asked in the
morning.

"Yes, Grandfather. You will see."
Young Wolf put his hands on
Red Wind's back.

"May I get on?" he asked.

"Nnnnn-hhhhh," said Red Wind.

"That means yes," Young Wolf told his
grandfather.

Then he gave a little jump and got his
arms across her back.

"Hoh," he said in a deep voice.

Red Wind turned her head and looked
at him. But she did not move.

Slowly he p-u-l-l-e-d himself up.

"Now, one leg over...and I'm on!"

His grandfather smiled.

Day after day Grandfather He-Bear taught Young Wolf to ride like a warrior. How to lean forward or back to make Red Wind go or stop. How to press with his knees to make her turn.

Young Wolf learned quickly. And so did Red Wind. She was smart, just as he thought.

His grandfather made a loop of horsehair. Then he braided the two ends into Red Wind's mane.

"Now you can ride on her side," he said. "Her body will protect you in battle."

"And I can shoot arrows across her back like a real warrior," said Young Wolf.

He put the loop over his head and arm.

"Watch me, Grandfather."

But before Young Wolf could try,
Little Big Mouth galloped by.

"Watch *me*, Baby Wolf."

He leaned into the loop and clung with
his legs. He aimed.

Twang! His arrow flew straight and hit the target.

"Let's see you do *that*!" he yelled.

"Let's show him, Red Wind," Young Wolf said. He leaned forward.

Red Wind sprang into a gallop.
Young Wolf let himself slip to her side.
He gripped with his legs and feet.

Then he held his bow steady across
her back.

"May my arrow have eyes," he said.

But Red Wind stumbled.

Young Wolf's arrow flew wide of the
target.

He pulled himself up on her back. "Hoh, Red Wind."

When she stopped, he jumped off. He felt up and down her leg.

"Don't worry," he told her. "Your leg is not broken."

Little Big Mouth yelled, "Get yourself a war horse."

"Let him talk," Young Wolf said to his mare.

4
Apaches!

It was the moon of painted leaves.

Young Wolf lay on his bed. He watched the smoke curl up to the smoke hole.

Voice of the Sunrise sat by the fire sewing beads on a new pair of moccasins.

"When will Father return?" asked Young Wolf.

"Not for several days. Not until he finds a herd of buffalo for the fall hunt," she said.

Young Wolf got up.

"The night is cold," he said. "I will cover Red Wind."

He placed a buffalo robe over the mare's back.

"Good night, my friend. May you dream of a warm spring day."

He tied her rope to his wrist while she nuzzled him.

Then he crawled under the bottom of the tepee and into his bed.

"Red Wind will stay warm now," he said. He pulled the robe up to his chin.

"Good night, Young Wolf," said Voice of the Sunrise. She put down her sewing and got into bed.

"Good night, Mother."

Young Wolf closed his eyes and soon fell asleep.

He awoke suddenly.

"What was that?" he asked.

"I heard nothing," said his mother.

He felt a tug on the rope and heard
Red Wind stomp her hoof.

Young Wolf crawled from his bed. He peeked under the tepee.

"What is it, Red Wind?" he whispered. "Why are you pulling on your rope?"

But this time the mare did not look at him when he talked. She looked toward the creek. Her ears stood up straight.

"I'm going out," Young Wolf said. "To see what is the matter with her."

"Be careful, my son," said Voice of the Sunrise.

Young Wolf crept outside. He looked where Red Wind was looking. In the meadow he saw something move—two dark shadows near the herd of horses.

Apaches! thought Young Wolf. They have come to steal our horses. I must warn the village.

He untied the rope and put his hand on Red Wind's back. "Hoh," he whispered.

Red Wind became still.

Young Wolf mounted without a sound. He leaned forward and Red Wind bolted off.

"Apaches! Apaches!" he cried.
Through the village he raced.
Warriors rushed out of their tepees
with bows in hand.

"Where, Young Wolf?" they shouted.

"There," he yelled, pointing toward
the meadow.

The warriors leaped onto their horses.

"After them!" they yelled. "They're heading for the creek."

Young Wolf rode with the warriors.

"Look! There they go!" he shouted. "On the other side."

They chased the Apaches until they disappeared into the hills.

Then the war chief called a halt. All the warriors gathered around him. Little Big Mouth was there too.

Chief Black Moon put his hand on Young Wolf's shoulder.

"You saved our horses, Young Wolf."

"It was Red Wind," the boy answered. "She warned me."

"Then you should be proud of her," said Black Moon. "She will make a good horse for a young warrior."

Not a single word came from Little Big Mouth's big mouth.

Young Wolf stroked his mare's neck.

"You are the smartest, most beautiful horse in the village."

"Nnnnn-hhhhh," said Red Wind.

And that means yes.